SECRET BATTLES

Algerina Pringle

Copyright © 2025 by **Algerina Pringle**

All rights reserved.

This book or any portion thereof may not be reproduced or used in any manner whatsoever without the express written permission of the publisher except for the use of brief quotations in a book review.

Printed in the United States of America

First Edition, 2025

PAPERBACK ISBN: 979-8-3485-4129-3

EBOOK ISBN: 979-8-3485-4130-9

Red Pen Edits and Consulting, LLC

www.redpeneditsllc.com

TABLE OF CONTENTS

DEDICATIONS 1

INTRODUCTION 3

CHAPTER ONE
Hidden In Plain Sight 5

CHAPTER TWO
Out Of Sync 13

CHAPTER THREE
The Fading Bond 19

CHAPTER FOUR
Forsaken 27

CHAPTER FIVE
Shadows Of The Past 33

CHAPTER SIX

Finding Peace In The Midst Of Bitterness 41

CHAPTER SEVEN

A Fractured Faith 49

CHAPTER EIGHT

Functioning In Dysfunction 57

CHAPTER NINE

Unmasking My Authenticity 63

CHAPTER TEN

A Love Like None Other 75

RESOURCES 81

ABOUT THE AUTHOR 83

Dedications

To those who carry the weight of unseen battles and to those who bury the emotions that whisper and rage within,

May this book be a gentle hand reaching into your hidden spaces, a reminder that you are not alone in your struggles.

May you find within these pages a reflection of your own journey, a validation of your pain, and a beacon of hope illuminating the path toward healing.

Lastly, may you discover, as I did, the strength and peace that comes from surrendering your secret battles to the One who sees and loves you completely.

Introduction

The air crackles with unspoken truths. We walk among each other, draped in the illusion of composure, while beneath the surface, a silent war rages. "Secret Battles" is not a tale of distant heroes, but a mirror reflecting the landscape of your own heart and the terrain of struggles fought in the quietest corners of your being. For years, I believed in the myth of self-sufficiency, navigating life's treacherous currents with a clenched fist and an unyielding will. My emotions, once vibrant companions, became silent adversaries, their battles waged in the shadows, leaving me adrift in a sea of weariness. The world, blinded by the facade I so carefully constructed, saw only a semblance of strength. But within, a tempest raged, a desperate yearning for a peace that eluded my grasp.

This book is a stripping away of pretense, a raw and honest testament to the vulnerability we so often conceal. It's a journey from the barren landscape of self-made solutions to the fertile ground of surrender, where I discovered the solace of divine grace.

"Secret Battles" is an invitation, a gentle nudge, to lay down your own hidden burdens, to seek the One who sees, knows, and heals, and to find that true victory lies not in solitary combat but in a victorious alliance with God.

Chapter One
HIDDEN IN PLAIN SIGHT

As a young child growing up in poverty, you don't want to be seen or even noticed. The hard fact is that you lacked what others had the best of. From clothing to living standards, and even how others were raised, there was a defined line of distinction. How can living in a two-parent household still create a sense and feeling of an absent parent? "Just because you're there, doesn't mean you're there". I know that my parents did the best that they could with what they had readily accessible to them.

As far as I can remember in my adolescent years, we've always lived in the same neighborhood. I can remember these run-down apartments with two bedrooms and one bathroom. One bedroom was for my parents and the other bedroom was for the siblings. I shared the bedroom with two older brothers and a younger sister. There were two sets of bunk beds in the room. Momma pieced meals together, but she made sure we ate. It might not have been what we wanted, but we had something. She made sure we all had what we needed. I never felt close to any of my siblings growing up. Unfortunately, we were never taught or even shown how to build a close-knit relationship with one another. Don't get me wrong! We cared for each other. Well, for the most part. Each of us had our own separate space.

We had a lot of children in our neighborhood to play with. It was one of those neighborhoods where everyone knew everyone, but it wasn't the family-oriented type of neighborhood.

There was a routine. Like clockwork, on Fridays, seventy percent of the adults would be drunk drinking. Then the fights would start, police would be called, and we would be peeping out the windows watching what we called a good TV show. This was a never-ending cycle week after week. The children in the neighborhood would all come together at times to play tag and kickball, sit on the pump house, and play cards. We would have fun until that one bully started confusion and picked a fight with someone. In team sports and games, I would always be the last one to get picked. There was nothing cool about me and I didn't even try to fit in.

I literally lived out the scripture where it says *"the last shall be first, and the first last"* **(Matthew 20:16 KJV)**. I would feel sad and keep all my feelings and emotions to myself. I would cap and bottle up my emotions inside of me.

As a child, I felt lonely. I felt like I was different. I felt like no one would even understand me if

I tried to explain. So, what was the use? This is where I taught myself how to just hold everything inside.

Healing from the experiences of that little girl within can be a challenging but rewarding process. Acknowledge and validate your feelings. Accept your experiences. Understand that your feelings are valid and that you deserve to be seen and heard from as a child and even as an adult. Practice self-compassion. Treat yourself with kindness and understanding. Talk to someone. Share your feelings with a trusted source.

Not being noticed is a struggle that comes with internal battles that we secretly face within ourselves. It comes with dealing with loneliness and isolation and that brings along self-doubt and low self-esteem. You may begin feeling inadequate and worthless. Then, we create fear of rejection which prevents us from forming connections. These internal battles foster resentment and bitterness towards others who seem to have fulfilling relationships. It's important to remember that these internal battles are common and that you're not alone in facing them. By recognizing these challenges and taking steps to address them, you can overcome loneliness and isolation and build meaningful connections with others.

The struggles of feeling unnoticed can happen in various settings and circumstances such as the workplace, in a marriage, as a child, or whatever challenges that life presents.

Here is some encouragement that I would like to share with you.

You are seen even when it feels like no one notices.

You matter.

Your presence, thoughts, and feelings all have value.

You are a unique masterpiece, and your story is worth telling.

Remember, sometimes the quietest people have the loudest hearts. Your strength lies in your resilience and your ability to persevere. Don't let the noise of others' lives drown out your own.

You are worthy of love, connections, and recognition. Keep shining your light, even in the darkest times.

You are not alone.

EXPRESS YOURSELF

SECRET BATTLES

Chapter Two

OUT OF SYNC

In my early teenage years, my parents purchased a new double wide trailer. In those days, if you purchased some land and put a trailer on it, you were considered big time. Unfortunately, we were still in the same neighborhood. The land they purchased was right across the street from the apartments. So, our environment didn't change – only our physical address changed. The girls had a room and the boys had another room. When it was time to clean our room, we bickered about cleaning our halves of the room. My mom never allowed friends to come over to stay and we weren't allowed to stay over at their homes. I only had one particular friend growing up. Other than that, I was to myself. One of my older brothers and I could never get alone. We would fuss all the time. He would pick at me because I didn't have friends. I wasn't cool and popular like him. Everyone knew me as their sister. My brother constantly picked and teased me. One day, he messed with me so much, I grabbed a knife from the kitchen and chased him around the house. Of course, our parents weren't home. My brother was so mean to me. It's a pretty sad reality when your bully is your very own brother. He didn't like me, and I didn't like him. I didn't have anywhere to go or anyone that I could express my feelings to. I didn't even know how to express them. I wrote a note about how I didn't want to live anymore. I don't know where I put it so that it could be found. That brother found it, and it just added fuel to the fire for him to tease me even more. I never told my mom or anyone about it. I just bottled it up inside of me. What was the use? I felt no one would understand. I felt misunderstood, and unloved. I was hurting because I felt less than who I was.

Feeling misunderstood can be a deeply isolating experience, often leading to secret battles that can take a toll on your mental and emotional well-being. When you're feeling that you're struggling with being misunderstood, become self-aware and self-accepting to help yourself move forward. Understand yourself. Spend time reflecting on your thoughts, feelings, and behavior. Embrace your individuality by recognizing that being different is okay. Practice self-compassion. Be kind to yourself and avoid self-criticisms.

Growing up misunderstood can be a painful experience. Misunderstanding can lead to a range of emotional distress, such as sadness, anger, frustration, and anxiety. The secret battles that we face can be challenging while trying to press our way through life not knowing that the secrets are grounded at the root of our heart.

Oftentimes, when dealing with certain circumstances, we wonder why things are happening the way that they are. Remember, it's okay to feel misunderstood, but it's more important to not let it define you. By developing self-awareness, practicing effective communication, building strong relationships, and seeking professional help, you can overcome the challenges of being misunderstood and live a fulfilling life.

If you're struggling with being misunderstood allow me to encourage you. Many people feel misunderstood at times. Your feelings are valid, and your expressions are real. Your worth isn't determined by the understanding of others. You are unique, and your perspective is valuable. Keep being you even if it means standing out. Your authenticity is your strength. Don't let the misunderstandings dim your light. Keep shining brightly, and eventually, people will see the true you. You're capable of amazing things, and your time to shine will come.

EXPRESS YOURSELF

18 | SECRET BATTLES

Chapter Three

THE FADING BOND

My brother wasn't just a sore in my behind. He was hanging around with the wrong crowd and things began to get worst with him. My mom ended up sending him to another state to stay with some family members to give him a better chance at life. Now, maybe I can breathe. By this time, we had another little brother added to the patch, but he was just a baby. So, there were no issues with that.

We had some new neighbors that moved into the lot next door. I found a new best friend. We were close. At this point, I was in junior high school. I wasn't into having any boyfriends. I was focused on school. My friend had a boyfriend and you know how that goes. They introduced me to one of their friends. So, I met this dude. He was cool. We chopped it up and became really good friends. That's it. We spent most of the time just conversing over the telephone. It was cool just having that person to talk to about life issues, to vent, and to encourage each other. We cut up and acted silly which was a good outlet for me. *Laughter is always a good way to release the tension of stress.* This went on for a couple of years. He went to a different school. So, we really didn't see each other a lot. One day, for some reason, he came up to my school. By this time, I was in high school and driving. We went to the mall. As time continued, we became closer. Eventually, it grew into something more serious, and we started dating. Soon after that, I graduated. We were just living and enjoying life as young adults. I became pregnant. It wasn't planned but, it happened. That's when things took a turn in our relationship. He felt like he didn't want the responsibility of a child. He began pushing me away and started distancing himself from me. That left me feeling confused, regretful, and blaming myself for opening up to someone. The feeling of loneliness arose. Being misunderstood hovered over me once again. So, here I am bottling up more feelings and emotions.

Healing from betrayal and abandonment can be a painful process. Coping through involves acknowledging and processing your emotions. Allow yourself to feel and don't suppress your emotions like anger, sadness, or betrayal. Journaling is a great technique to write about your feelings to help gain clarity and express yourself. Spend time with supportive people. Surround yourself with positive influences. Assess and understand the situation. Avoid the victim mentality. Take responsibility for your own well-being. Learn from the experience. Reflect on what you can learn from the situation. Set boundaries. Protect yourself from further hurt. Focus on the future. Let go of the past. Don't dwell on what happened. Embrace new opportunities.

Focus on positive experiences and relationships. Build your self-worth. Remind yourself of your strengths and accomplishments.

Dealing with abandonment and betrayal can trigger a range of secret battles. With self-doubt, you may question your worthiness of love and connections to others. With anger and resentment, you may feel angry at the person who betrayed you or resentful of the situation. You may feel sadness, as if you've lost a part of yourself. You may face the fear of trusting others. Then, there's the guilt and shame causing you to blame yourself for the situation or feel ashamed of your vulnerability. It's important to recognize these secret battles and begin to practice self-compassion. It's okay to feel these emotions by acknowledging them and seeking support. You can work through them and emerge stronger.

When facing the battles of abandonment and betrayal, I would love to encourage you! You are stronger and braver than you think. While it might feel like the world has shattered, this too shall pass. You have the power to heal, to grow, and to rebuild. Every pain you feel is a testament to the depth of love you once shared. Don't let it consume you. Let it fuel your journey towards self-discovery and resilience. You deserve love, respect, and loyalty. Don't settle for anything less. Keep your heart open but be discerning. You'll find people who truly value you. Surround yourself with positive influences - people who uplift and support you. Lean on them during tough times, and celebrate your victories with them. You are not alone. Many have walked this path before you, and many will walk it after.

EXPRESS YOURSELF

Chapter Four

FORSAKEN

During my pregnancy, I experienced moments of loneliness and shame. Thank God for my mother! She did not give up on me when she found out I was pregnant. She was with me every step of the way. I only had one set of living grandparents, my paternal grandparents. Both of my maternal grandparents passed away when my mother was a young child. Once my grandparents and aunts found out about my pregnancy, they pretty much disowned me because I was having a baby out of wedlock. All kinds of negative talk came from that. They thought I was going to put the baby off on my mom. At this point my whole world was crumbling right before me. *"Your circumstances doesn't define your character nor your future"*. As time went on, this created a wedge and caused distance in our family. I loved my family. This was a hurt that I carried for years - thirteen years to be exact. There was no communication. I gave birth to my handsome baby boy with no father in sight. His dad still had no interest in stepping up to the plate. I was focused on my baby. I did what I had to do to take care of my baby. I cut all ties with his father, moved on and didn't look back. I worked two jobs while living with my parents. My mom only watched my son when I had to work, and I paid her weekly for doing so. If I wanted to go out, I paid her extra. I didn't mind because that was my son and my responsibility. I did more than pay for childcare expenses. There were times when I would put food in the house and pay for utilities such as the electricity, phone and water bills. That was never a problem. I was always good with saving my money. My level of financial responsibility positioned me as a resource for my mother when she needed help. During this time of my life, I felt all of my previous emotions. The feelings got more intense, but because of what was spoken over me, I was more determined than ever to do the best that I could with what I had.

Being determined while hurting is a testament to human resilience. It's about finding the strength to keep moving forward, even when it feels impossible. Navigate this challenging period by acknowledging your pain. Allow yourself to feel. Don't suppress your emotions. Cultivate a positive, mindset. Practice gratitude focus on the positive aspects of your life. Challenge negative thoughts. Replace them with positive affirmations. Visualize success. Imagine yourself overcoming challenges and achieving your goals.

Healing takes time. Be patient with yourself and don't give up on your dreams. By staying determined and practicing self-care, you can overcome any obstacle and come out stronger than ever. When facing tough times, I want to encourage you. Remember, every storm passes. This moment of difficulty is a temporary chapter, not the whole story. You've faced challenges before, and you've come out stronger. This time will be no different. Keep your head held high. Your resilience is unwavering. Every obstacle you overcome makes you stronger. Don't let setbacks define you; let them fuel your determination. You've got the strength within you to weather this storm. Keep pushing forward, one step at a time. You've got this!

EXPRESS YOURSELF

SECRET BATTLES

Chapter Five

SHADOWS OF THE PAST

After I had my son, I started working two jobs: one at a restaurant and the other in retail. After working in retail for about a year, I was offered a full-time position. The downside was that I had to drive forty-five minutes to and from work each day. I was willing to do whatever I had to do in order to advance myself financially and provide a better life for myself and my son,. After a few years, I quit the restaurant job. I was content with life. I wanted more but I was unsure about what I wanted more of. However, I was content. One week, I went on a vacation. When I returned, there was this new employee. We both arrived at the same time and waited at the door before the store opened. I continued through the day as normal and so did he. Then, I found out that he was asking other co-workers about me. Then, one day, he approached me, and we exchanged numbers. He seemed to be a good dude. We hung out for a while and then started dating on a more serious level. He took my son as his own. He didn't have any children. He stepped up and took on that responsibility. That was a huge plus in my eyes. We were bonding as a family. Four years later, I moved out my parents' house and got my first place with him. I was about to have another baby boy. He was so excited. I was excited for the reaction he gave. Things were great or at least I thought they were.

I started noticing some red flags after a while such as random phone calls, staying away from home longer, and always needing to go somewhere. Come to find out, he was still involved with the person who was supposed to be his ex. Apparently, she was never out of the picture. After giving birth to my second son, he decided that he wanted to be with her, but he was going to still take care of the boys. He packed up some of his things and left. He left some things behind so that he could have access. Being in love, I gave him that access. This experience brought along a lot of trust issues. It brought on a feeling of worthlessness along with the secret battles that I already had buried inside.

Dealing with trust issues can be challenging, but it's definitely possible to overcome them.

Here's an approach that can help you navigate through this process.

Acknowledge and understand the root causes.

Why do you feel this way?

Reflect on past experiences. Identify specific events or relationships that have contributed to your trust issues.

Were there patterns of betrayal, deception, or abandonment?

Consider your attachment style. Understanding your attachment style can provide insights into how you form and maintain relationships.

Are there insecurities, feelings of anxiousness, and/or a void you're trying to fill?

Having trust issues can create significant secret battles within. The fear of vulnerability and trusting someone requires opening up, which can be terrifying if you've been hurt in the past. You might battle with the fear of being hurt again, leading to self-protection and the avoidance of intimacy. With constant vigilance and suspicion, you may find yourself constantly scanning for signs of betrayal or deception. This can lead to anxiety, exhaustion, and strained relationships as you struggle to relax and truly enjoy connections.

These secret battles can be exhausting and emotionally draining. If you're struggling with trust issues, let me encourage you. It's important to be gentle with yourself. Trust is a gift, and it takes time to build. Don't rush the process. Start small and gradually open yourself up to others. You deserve to have healthy and fulfilling relationships. Don't let past hurts define your future. You are worthy of trust and love. Treat yourself with kindness. Be patient with yourself as you work through these challenges. Forgive yourself. It's okay to have and acknowledge your trust issue without self-blame. You've got this. You are worthy. You are loved. You are enough. Now just believe it for yourself.

EXPRESS YOURSELF

Chapter Six

FINDING PEACE IN THE MIDST OF BITTERNESS

He was playing the back-and-forth game and I was no longer in a happy place. I still loved him and I wanted our family to work, but he wasn't ready to be committed to one relationship. This created tension between his ex and me. Neither of us were willing to cut ties and let him go. This led to constant drama between all of us. It took a real, life-changing event to happen before I realized that this relationship was toxic and would never be anything fulfilling to my life. He ended up going to prison for fifteen years. I visited him every weekend and as much as I could until it clicked in my head to simply stop.

I finally accepted that the relationship was over. I wanted to maintain a stable home environment for me and my children. I moved into an apartment with my boys. When I had to work, I would drop them off at my mom's. Then, I started attending a church every Sunday. My parents never attended church regularly. They always sent us to church with the children of their close friends. Out of all of my siblings, I was the only one that continued to go to church. Whether it was with a friend or just randomly, I would go to church. I never got involved. I would just go to church, sit in the back and when church was over, I would leave. There was no communication and no fellowshipping.

Life was hard as a single parent, but I kept pushing through. I never pushed for child support. To me, it was too much of a headache and not worth dealing with it. When I cut ties, I cut ties. I refused to be bound by these guys over a few dollars. Because of that decision, I spent many nights crying and wondering how ends were going to be met. Through it all, the bills got paid and were never late. One of my biggest accomplishments was in the purchase of my first house. Do you want to know about discipline and hard work? That's exactly what it took to save money over a long period of time. With the odds against me, I did it! I was single mother, but I did it! I was a young, black female, but I did it! Even in the face of adversity and some secret battles of bitterness as it relates to trusting me, I made my peace and pushed forward with a greater determination. By this time in my life, I had lost all trust in people. If I needed it or wanted it, the ball was in my court to make it happen. There were moments of defeat, but I had no choice but to push through.

When feeling defeated, you may face a range of secret battles: self-doubt, hopelessness, anger, and frustration, shame and guilt, and apathy. Apathy can set in making it difficult to find the energy or motivation to try again. These secret battles can create a vicious cycle making it difficult to recover from defeat and move forward. If you find yourself battling with defeat, shift your mindset to navigate into a position of determination and focus on your own personal growth. Determination is a powerful force that can have a profound impact on your life. Determination provides you with the inner strength to persevere through challenges, setbacks, and failures. It fuels the resilience needed to bounce back and keep moving forward. Each time you overcome a challenge through determination, you build self-belief and confidence in your abilities. Determination acts as an internal motivator driving you to push your limits and strive for excellence.

I encourage you to overcome that defeat and cultivate determination. Defeat is not the end of the road, it's a detour. You have the strength within you to find a new path and reach your destination. Every obstacle you overcome makes you stronger. Remember your past successes? You've overcome obstacles before, and you can do it again. Every setback offers valuable insights. Use the experience to grow and improve. Don't let this defeat define you. Believe in yourself. You are capable of achieving great things. Keep pushing forward, one step at a time. You have the power to rise above this and achieve your dreams.

EXPRESS YOURSELF

Chapter Seven

A FRACTURED FAITH

By now, a few years have passed and I am content with the routine of my life. I can remember my mom having a cookout on Labor Day. My mom loved to feed people. If you stopped by, you got a plate. You don't hear me talk about my dad a lot. My dad was a quiet, stay-to-self type of guy. One of my brother's friends was at the cookout and we were all playing cards. It was a good time of laughs and fun as always. When I got home, my brother asked if it was ok to give out my number. "I guess. What the heck?!" Why did I do that?

He became so aggravating. When I got home, he was cutting my grass. When I came home in the evening, he was bringing us pizza. I mean. It was a nice gesture and all, but I don't like being bothered. I was in a good space, by myself. He was so persistent and he did not take his foot off the gas. This man knew what he wanted. I ended up giving in to his pursuit and we started dating. He welcomed me with open arms into his world of bikers. This environment was filled with fun, riding, and a lot of partying. It felt so good to be out and enjoy myself. I started to come out of my shell more. This was a great outlet for me. My life was filled with work, church and taking my boys to visit their father in prison.

After a year or so, I can vividly remember a Saturday before Mother's Day. I was making plans to go to the prison that Sunday morning. I took my mom her gift on that Saturday. She was her normal vibrant self while frying chicken and moving around the house. I gave my mom her gift and headed home. When I got home, I sat in the car listening to some gospel music and my phone started ringing. My sister was calling me to say that something was wrong with mom. I immediately rushed back to my mom's house. When I got there, the ambulance had already transported her to the hospital so I drive there as fast as I could. We found out that mom had a major stroke. It was necessary for her to be flown to another hospital for care. She laid unresponsive in the hospital for almost a week until the doctors could drain some of the fluid from her brain. She was in a critical condition on a ventilator and with a feeding tube.

The hospital was about 15 minutes from the job where I was working. I went to the hospital everyday during my lunch and when I got off. I prayed for healing. My faith was no where as strong as it is now, but I knew that if I asked God to do it, He would do it. My mom gained some strength, but she never came off the ventilator or feeding tube. She couldn't talk or walk. We could read her lips, but she would get frustrated when we couldn't understand her. After six months in the hospital, she was sent home to be comfortable while continuing the journey of gaining strength. After about a month and half, she passed away. When she passed, I felt like a piece of me left as well. Even worse, I felt that God didn't hear me. I started navigating through life with a nonchalant, don't care attitude. I stopped going to church. I turned my back on God and the many people that I felt betrayed me. I lost all faith in God. Mr. Pringle had been by my side every step of the way and I was so grateful for his faithfulness to me. We got married almost two years later. Getting through the grieving process takes time, but life seemed to have been flowing into place. The passing of my mom opened up a line of communication with my grandparents and aunts again.

If you struggle with your faith, it's a normal part of the human experience. The secret battles you may face include:

- Feelings of anger at God for perceived injustices,

- Unanswered prayers, or
- The suffering in the world.

This can lead to:

- Questioning the existence of God,
- Questioning the truthfulness of religious teachings, and
- Questioning the meaning of life.

Overcoming the secret battles you may face with struggles of your faith is a deeply personal journey. Identify the root of doubt. Writing down your thoughts and feelings can help you understand and process your doubts. Talk to a trusted source.

Life is a journey with a lot of uncertainty. Faith is not always about having all the answers. It's about trusting in something greater than yourself, even when you don't fully understand. The word of God says in **Isaiah 55:8**, *"For my thoughts are not your thoughts, neither are your ways my ways, saith the LORD."* Be gentle with yourself during this time of struggle. Remember God's love is unconditional and that He is always there for you, even in your doubts. Even if you feel distant from God, continue to engage in prayer. It can be a way to express your doubts, frustrations, and longings.

EXPRESS YOURSELF

SECRET BATTLES

Chapter Eight

FUNCTIONING IN DYSFUNCTION

I truly felt like I married my best friend. We had a baby girl. Things were looking up. I was able to talk to him about things that I was unable to talk to anyone else about. I was able to express my feelings to my husband. We have had a lot of great times together. He invited me into his world with open arms, and I met a lot of great people along the way. Our relationship was very calming. We have had disagreements, but never any arguments. There were no insecurities, just living, partying, drinking, and doing what seemed to be enjoying life. It was nothing better than ole cocktails.

Although everything was going well, I kept feeling this inner urge. I didn't know what it was, so I ignored it. At least I tried to ignore it. This feeling kept rising and nudging on me for years. Then, on New Year's Eve 2018, my sister, her husband, my husband and I were sitting at the dining room table having drinks. Something came over me. I started crying and confessing that I didn't want to continue maneuvering through like I was. I needed God in my life. From that moment forward, I would follow God. Something shifted in me that night. The urge to seek God more became a greater desire for me.

This was an unexpected, divine intervention by God. This was God's miraculous and surprising intervention in human form. God can and does act in ways that defy human understanding or expectations. In most cases, it happens in our greatest time of need and despair. God knows the things that we have no knowledge of. I thank

God for intervening and saving me from any destruction that lies ahead of me.

One night, I was dreaming. I kept hearing over and over, *"For I know the thoughts that I think toward you, saith the Lord, thoughts of peace, and not of evil, to give you an expected end."* **(Jeremiah 29:11)** That verse sat in my spirit long after the dream. I contained little faith as I was just beginning to take this walk with Christ seriously. I was like a newborn baby seeking to learn more and more, I was hungry to learn and draw closer to Christ. I became connected to three powerful men and women of God. They were selfless in embracing me and teaching me the word of God. They were patient with me. They were kind and met me right where I was. I had millions of questions. I thought I was aggravating them, but they took the time to break my questions down so I could understand them. God will give you who you need, when you need them. Day by day my faith was growing. I wanted to learn more and more.

Divine intervention is seen as a manifestation of God's love, power, and faithfulness. It's a testament to God's active involvement in the world and his willingness to intervene in human lives. Regardless of one's personal beliefs, the concept of unexpected divine intervention offers a powerful message of hope and the possibility of something greater than ourselves. It's a reminder that even in the face of adversity, there's always the potential for something extraordinary to occur.

EXPRESS YOURSELF

Chapter Nine

UNMASKING MY AUTHENTICITY

I was diligently seeking after God. My desire to know Him more, and to learn more about myself was very personal and intentional for me. I'll be honest. I stumbled back a few times and didn't understand or know my purpose, but my trust in God was growing. Some things started to adjust in my life. I didn't have a desire to hang out. So, I stopped. This was a personal journey. I didn't expect my husband to change his desires for what I was feeling. He continued to go out. I didn't have any issues with it. This became our new norm. I went to church. He went to parties.

As your faith begins to grow, there will be tests. I started having these pressure headaches. They weren't like other headaches. I ignored it for as long as I could until the pain got more and more intense. They started interfering with my daily life routines. Normal routines and actions that we take for granted, gave me pain. When I laughed, it hurt. When I bent over to tie my shoes, there was pain. I went to my primary physician multiple times before being diagnosed with cerebella tonsillar ectopia also referred to as char malformation. I was referred to a neurosurgeon and his immediate resolution was brain surgery. There were no recommended medications to treat this disorder. My first sense of relief came when I knew what was going on. Being in the dark or unsure when it comes to your health is a lonely place. All I could think about was my mother. Vibrant one moment and then, a stroke the next moment. I depended on my circle of friends to pray for me. That helped to build my strength.

I gave the situation to God. Without a shadow of doubt, He was in control. I believed that everything was going to be just fine. On May 4, 2021, I had my surgery and everything went just fine. Two weeks after an intense brain surgery, I was out walking and talking without skipping a beat. God is so amazing! Two months after my surgery, I got baptized. I was more in love with God than ever before.

Developing myself became my priority. I attended personal and professional development events, empowerment events, revivals, and mentorship programs. Seeking God is still my goal. I had a lot of wrongs to make right. Casting down loneliness; filling my surroundings with the presence of God. Casting down bitterness and betrayal; filling myself with love. I could feel the love that God had for me and that was an emotion that I had never felt before. That was something that I never wanted to depart from. Cultivating self-love is crucial. It allows you to recognize your own worth and value - dependent of others' actions. I was learning to let go of not being recognized and being misunderstood; filling myself with self-worth. Recognizing your own worth builds confidence and allows you to navigate social situations with greater ease and authenticity. Acknowledge and appreciate your unique talents, abilities, and perspectives.

I was more determined than ever to become the best version of myself. When my determination collided with my faith, I became unstoppable. However, this is where the enemy tried to rise up against me. It started with the small things such as maintenance issues in the house, and automobile issues. When I fixed one, another issue started. I managed a retail store and there were issues on the job. It was like a snowball effect. The more a snowball is rolled, the more snow it accumulates and the bigger it gets. For those of you who have ever gone camping, when you see baby cubs, it is not the time to pet them. The momma bear is not too far away. Momma bears are fierce and very protective. The enemy tried to attack my children. That's my weak spot. This attack hit me like a ton of bricks on my chest. I couldn't breathe. My flesh was weak. The first thing I could do was call someone who I could lean on. Knowing that you have that type of support and guidance from trusted sources can boost your confidence and empower you to make bold decisions and/or uplift you in your time of need. It took more strength and more pressing, but I trusted God throughout that situation. The trust that was faded and diminished by my past circumstances was restored. I trusted myself, my abilities, and in the divine support that was available to me. My restored faith gave me the courage to step outside my comfort zone, take risks, and pursue dreams.

Remember that snowball? Well, it was still forming and it splatted all over my home. My marriage was now under attack. We had been living two separate lifestyles. In **Corinthians 7:14**, it says, 'For the unbelieving husband is sanctified by the wife, *and the unbelieving wife is sanctified by the* *husband"*. I know the word, but I felt like I would do more harm than good if I tried to persuade him into my lifestyle. If he was going to change, it had to be by the hand of God. I joined this local church. For the first time, in a long time, I was involved and active. I was attending Sunday School, worship service, and bible study every week. We started having arguments (previously, it was just disagreements) about this church. His health started to decline, but the arguments continued. As the submissive wife, I stopped attending that church in hopes that he would find a church for us to attend together. A month went by, and we were sitting at the house on Sundays. Two weeks later and still, there was no church. After much prayer and fasting, God instructed me to return to the church that I stopped attending. I was glad to be back, but the attacks intensified.

My husband's health continued to decline. He had three major surgeries, endured a two-week hospital stay and then, he was referred to a rehabilitation center for a month. Daily, I would pick up our daughter and visit with him. Without explanation and with no definitive answers from tests results, his health declined even more. During his last week in the facility, he said that he had an encounter with God. He made a promise to God that he would get into church. When he got home, the sickness stopped. The pain was there, but the sickness stopped. When he recovered, he made his way to church.

He started attending church regularly. He got baptized, joined the church, and he serves actively.

God is so faithful!

> *"But as for you, ye thought evil against me; but God meant it unto good, to bring to pass, as it is this day, to save much people alive."*
>
> **Genesis 50:20**

There is an anointing when you know, that you know, what the Lord has instructed you to do. You have to know when it doesn't look right to others. You have to know when folks start talking about you. "Oh! She must have done something before." There will be times when you don't understand yourself, but when you trust and believe, according to **Hebrews 13:5**, God *"will never leave thee, nor forsake thee."* I exercised my holy boldness in conversation with God. There were many times that I told God that I knew He didn't bring me this far to leave me here.

There's no need to hold on to the bitterness of what happened.

> *"Cast your care upon the Lord and He will sustain you; He will never let the righteous be shaken."*
>
> **Psalms 55:22**

> *"Faithful is he who calls you,*
> *who also will do it."*
>
> **Thessalonians 5:24**

This verse assures us that God is faithful to His word and will complete the work He has begun in us. "Hold on to God's unchanging hand."

In all things, seek after God!

> *"But seek ye first the kingdom of God and His righteousness; and all these things shall be added unto you."*
>
> **Matthew 6:33**

EXPRESS YOURSELF

Chapter Ten

A LOVE LIKE NONE OTHER

God's love isn't based on our performance or worthiness. It's a constant, unwavering love that He extends to everyone. God loves you deeply and unconditionally, just as you are.

> *"For God so loved the world, that He gave His only begotten Son, that whosoever believes in Him should not perish, but have everlasting life."*
>
> **John 3:16**

The gift of grace is undeserved favor. It's God's freely given love and forgiveness, even when we fall short. God's grace is sufficient for you. It's through His grace that we are saved and made whole.

> *"But He said to me, 'My grace is sufficient for you, for my power is made perfect in weakness.' Therefore I will boast all the more gladly of my weakness, so that the power of Christ may rest on me."*
>
> **2 Corinthians 12:9**

God's love has the power to heal brokenness, restore relationships, and bring about profound transformation in our lives. You need to experience the transformative power of God's love in your life. It can heal your wounds and bring you everlasting peace. I encourage you to reflect on your relationship with God and consider the implications of God's love in your life.

> *"Come to me, all you who are weary and burdened, and I will give you rest."*
>
> **Matthew 11:28**

If you struggle in your relationship with God…

If you haven't considered a relationship with God…

If you have a relationship with God, but want to draw closer to Him…

I always encourage you to start reading the book of John so that God can show you and you can feel the love that God has for you. God is longing for you to feel His presence all over you.

God is waiting on you!

EXPRESS YOURSELF

Resources

Holy Bible, King James Version (KJV)

Holy Bible, New International Version (NIV)

About The Author

ALGERINA PRINGLE:

A Journey of Growth and Impact

Algerina Pringle is a wife, a mother, and a Certified John Maxwell Leadership Developer. At her core, she is deeply connected to the people she encounters. This connection inspires her to help them discover and reach their highest potential.

Algerina Pringle is the Founder and CEO of two organizations:
Transitioning Into Wholeness
and Vibrant Scents

Transitioning Into Wholeness is a non-profit organization that provides a platform for individuals to share their inspiring stories through our talk show. We also offer coaching and youth leadership development programs, empowering young people to become the leaders of tomorrow.

Vibrant Scents is a unique candle company that fosters connection. We invite friends, family, and colleagues to come together to create their own custom-scented candles, creating memorable experiences and fostering deeper relationships.

Algerina Pringle is a self-motivated individual with a thirst for knowledge and a passion for continuous growth. She believes in embracing the journey, recognizing that each day presents an opportunity for improvement. Stepping outside of her comfort zone is a constant in her life, as she strives to be all that God has called her to be.

Algerina Pringle is excited about her life's path knowing that every step and every connection contributes to a life of purpose and impact.

www.ingramcontent.com/pod-product-compliance
Lightning Source LLC
LaVergne TN
LVHW061040070526
838201LV00073B/5122